The Dinner Party

Also by Colleen Keating and published by Ginninderra Press

A Call To Listen (Shortlisted, Society of Women Writers NSW Book Awards 2016)

Fire on Water (Highly Commended, Society of Women Writers NSW Book Awards 2018; Nautilus Award – Silver 2017)

Hildegard of Bingen: A poetic journey (Winner, Poetry, and Winner, Non-fiction, Society of Women Writers NSW Book Awards 2020; Nautilus Award, Silver, 2019)

Desert Patterns (Highly Commended, Poetry, Society of Women Writers NSW Book Awards 2020)

Olive Muriel Pink: Her radical and idealistic life: A poetic journey (Highly Commended, Poetry, Society of Women Writers NSW Book Awards 2022)

Beachcomber

Soft Gaze, with Michael Keating (Picaro Poets)
Brush of Birds (Picaro Poets)
Landscapes of the Heart, with John Egan (Picaro Poets)
Shared Footprints, with Michael Keating (Picaro Poets)
Mood Indigo, with Pip Griffin (Picaro Poets)
Mists of Time, with Decima Wraxall (Pocket Poets)

Colleen Keating

The Dinner Party
A poetic response

Thanks

For their positive critique, affirmation and support as always, I would like to thank my writing and poetry network groups at Writing NSW and Rozelle Centre, and U3A poetry groups at Epping and Pennant Hills.

Thank you to Pip Griffin for her support and gracious ongoing edits of this work.
My loving appreciation to Michael for his constant presence and inspiration.

To my daughters, Elizabeth, Bernadine, Sarah-Clare and Jessica, daughters-in-law Amy and Anna, and granddaughters, Jacinta, Gemma and Eleanor.

To all women whose names remain unrecorded, unrecognised or forgotten, who died in childbirth, from witchcraft trials, in suffragette struggles, who put their life on the line, jammed a foot in a door, defied rules, refused to comply, broke glass ceilings and on whose shoulders we as women stand today.

The Dinner Party: A poetic response
ISBN 978 1 76109 530 6
Copyright © text Colleen Keating 2023
Cover image: Judy Chicago
The Dinner Party, 1974–79
Ceramic, porcelain, textile
576 × 576 in. (1463 × 1463 cm). Brooklyn Museum,
Gift of the Elizabeth A. Sackler Foundation, 2002.10
© Judy Chicago/Artist Rights Society (ARS) New York;
Photo © Donald Woodman/ARS NY

First published 2023 by
GINNINDERRA PRESS
PO Box 3461 Port Adelaide 5015
www.ginninderrapress.com.au

Contents

Restoring Women to History	9
Wing One: Prehistory to the Roman Empire	13
Primordial goddess	15
Fertile goddess	17
Ishtar	19
Kali	21
Snake Goddess	23
Sophia	25
Amazon	27
Hatshepsut	29
Judith	31
Sappho	34
Aspasia of Miletus	37
Boadaceia	39
Hypatia	41
Wing Two: Beginnings of Christianity to the Reformation	43
Marcella of Rome	45
Bridget	47
Theodora	49
Hrosvitha	52
Trota of Salerno	54
Eleanor of Aquitaine	56
Hildegard of Bingen	59
Petronilla de Meath	62
Christine de Pizan	64
Isabella d'Este	66
Regina, Elizabeth I	68
Artemisia Gentileschi	70
Anna Maria van Schurman	73

Wing Three: Beginning of the Women's Revolution	77
Anne Hutchinson	79
Sacajawea	82
Caroline Herschel	84
Mary Wollstonecraft	86
Sojourner Truth	89
Susan B. Anthony	91
Elizabeth Blackwell	94
Emily Dickinson	96
Ethyl Mary Smyth	99
Margaret Sanger	102
Natalie Barney	104
Virginia Woolf	106
Georgia O'Keeffe	108
Notes on the poems and women at the dinner party	111
Judy Chicago	140
Bibliography	141
Illustrations	144

'Afroditi, take the nectar
and delicately pour it into gold
wine cups and mingle joy with
our celebration.'
– Sappho

'Another world is not only possible, she is on her way.
On a quiet day I can hear her breathing.'
– Arundhati Roy

Once upon a time, when women were birds, there was the
simple understanding that to sing at dawn and to sing at
dusk was to heal the world through joy.
The birds still remember what we have forgotten,
that the world is meant to be celebrated.
– Terry Tempest Williams

Restoring Women to History

Welcome to our 2023 celebration – a dinner party, a poetic response to a universal dinner party.

Imagine the buzz of women from all over the Western world and all down the ages, colourful fashions, cultures, languages and imagine the sizzle and aromas of foods and the swapping of recipes, ideas, hints and stories. Just think of the after-parties as each spreads the word to celebrate unsung women back in their places right up till now, for women still today are having to put themselves on the line, call out treatment and celebrate their steps forward as they claim women's rights as human rights.

The Dinner Party is a 1978 landmark permanent installation of the American artist Judy Chicago. It is widely acclaimed as the first epic feminist art installation and takes pride of place in the Elizabeth A. Sackler Centre for Feminist Art, Brooklyn Museum, New York. A large triangular table for a ceremonial banquet, it is arranged for thirty-nine place settings with each side of the triangle measuring fifteen metres. It serves as a tribute to mythical, historic and forgotten women who deserve a seat at the table from the four thousand years of Western world history. On the tiles below are the names of nine hundred and ninety-nine more women who were also written out of history, forgotten or marginalised and on whose shoulders they stand.

In 2018, during the research for my book on Hildegard of Bingen, I came across the information about this amazing installation and the names of the many women down the ages of history being remembered and honoured. I was thrilled that Hildegard was included at *The Dinner Party* and it set me on a journey to research the other little known women so honoured.

Each woman commemorated at the table is designated a place setting. A china painted plate with a signature motif based on butterfly, flower and vulva forms is placed on an embroidered runner, with their name and icons of their personal and historical story. It acknowledges the long and interwoven history of women's accomplishment and succeeds in restoring women's heritage to our culture.

The research for *The Dinner Party* and the artistic work of Judy Chicago and her team has been hailed as a striking and powerful piece and a significant step on the road to recovery of herstory.

Since traditional history has avoided or suppressed women in history, the technique for feminist scholars has been to search for women everywhere, and to recreate historical periods and women's lifetimes as fully as possible – women first in their field who gave their life, suffered, broke barriers, knocked down walls, smashed glass ceilings, opened doors in some way for all of us.

It is only in the last couple of generations that history has been rewritten, consciously discovering and acknowledging the work of women from all fields of human endeavour.

Judy Chicago's words stun with their relevance today:

> Women have always made a significant contribution to the development of human civilisation, but have been consistently ignored, denied or trivialised.

In 2015, thirty-nine young artistic dancers visited the *The Dinner Party*. Each took a place at the table behind the names and place settings and danced, swayed, held hands and sang a celebratory ritual. A synergy of healing joy filled the room. It was as if the centuries of women represented were rising up to insist on freedom and equity for every woman on the planet.

Now, today, this book is a poetic response to the journey of women. I like to think of each one at the table, leaning into the conversation, nodding their affirmation as they celebrate their stories, their struggles and triumphs, and this moment of togetherness.

Enjoy getting to know more of the women on whose shoulders we stand.

Wing One
Prehistory to the Roman Empire

'The moon appeared in all her fullness and so the women took their place around the altar' – Sappho LP 154

Primordial goddess

Untethered from the bones of Khaos
Gaia, great feminine force
enlivens the cosmos.
Her heaving groans

birth the elements of mother earth.
With every lock of hair
she threads a web of life
and sings the earth alive.
Her mountainous breasts
nurture her creations
arms open, wide as millennia.

Her breath wrinkles the land
forming valleys for
gushing birth waters to flow.
Her feet dance the sun and stars to fire.

From ice-peaks of Mount Olympus
her gods pattern the seasons
and cycles of the moon
and like the sunflower
that turns with the sun
her body finds its rhythm.

Primordial goddess, we honour you
birther, creator, our matriarch.
We are handmaidens
sharing at your bridal feast.
Even as we each preside alone
you, mother goddess, give us your all –
your whole body and essence
spirited into the great Aum.

Your place setting with the feminine motif
of the coil, comfort of calfskins
gathering of cowry and clay
with stone-bead tools
reminds us from whence we come.
Welcome to our dinner party

Fertile goddess

Amid maypole ribbons and cascade of gowns
her fertility shines in sheaves of wheat
as yellow as her braided tresses swirling
in the golden runnels of Botticelli's *Venus*.
Her growing lushness gives life
to water, land and all creation.

When Hades abducts her daughter –
the beauty of spring
we taste her tears of grief
and a winter of barren earth
celebrate aromas of abundance
and harvest at her return.

She is the generous verdancy
of mother earth
the one who pulls a bucket up
from a long dark well
quenching thirst with cool clear water.

Sometimes as a shape-shifter
her Rubenesque breasts nourish
with the sweetness of mother's milk
laying a path through the sky.
Her fecund belly nurtures
gifts us our bleeding –
our hidden power in dark of moon.

Fertile goddess we drink from
the moss green of your eyes
falling to all as benevolence.

We, the everywoman –
knowing there is always a Hades
greedy to take your fertility
and leave a wasted earth
look to your vigilance.

Fertile goddess, your place setting
laid out on a coarse burlap
knitted from needles of cow femur
and wool spun on looms –
women's earliest tools
honours you, bounteous one.
Welcome to our dinner party.

Ishtar

Mistress of heaven
with wing-bearing arms
pectoral jewels
and ornate headdress, befitting
a priestess of divine powers
clothed in radiance
of the eight-pointed star
and claimed goddess of sexuality.

Not creator
more destroyer, slayer of the old –
unshakable, unyielding.
Always standing triumphant
heart lofty as the steel-grey sky
broad as the earth
standing in the paradox
between peace and war
standing in the liminal –
her descent into the underworld
and re-emergence
reminding us of love
where love is the battlefield.

Tear-blinded
we know that battlefield
where still today *counting dead women*
burdens our very soul.

Ishtar, your abrasive edges
cut lovers taken with abandonment
your honeyed mouth
turns venomous at a whim
we learn from you, sexual warrior.
Your geometrical place setting
from the Babylonian Ishtar Gate
with stepped levels of ziggurat
embroidered in brick stitch
shows us a multifaceted goddess.
Welcome to our dinner party.

Kali

Kali, fierce Hindu goddess
bewitcher of the Destructive Lord,
a fiery dancer
deeply feared, adored
forever blissful.

Like a thunderous wild storm
taking everything in its path
Kali is a wilful destroyer
her stance of fury
stamps deathly on ignorance.
With her multi-mighty arms
she transforms a female world.

There is no time to shrink before violence
no time to confuse exterior gain
or interior triumph
when women's power is assaulted.

Within her spirit we reclaim
a landscape where violence
is repudiated, not affirmed
demanding genders meet as equals
and female terms rescued from abuse

Kali, Valkyrie – dispenser of destiny
we accept your twofold image
of creator and destroyer.

Your place setting with blood red
and purple flames
leaps loudly from the needlework
like flayed skin
yet the core of your plate is filled with seeds
Does this not symbolise fecundity?

Kali, you the one that fires
feminine spirit.
Welcome to our dinner party.

Snake Goddess

From ancient mythic times
in labyrinthine palaces
a Snake Goddess emerged
honoured in frescoes
decorating vases, pots
in ivory, clay and *faïence* figures.

A bare-breasted goddess in
long flounced, bell-shaped skirt
tight bodice, low-cut
fastened at the waist
with *sejant* cat perched on her crown
snakes entwined around arms
upraised to embrace her priestess role
to encircle the Cretan world
as fate weaver.

Sometimes nurturer
fertility goddess
shedding the skin of old
honoured in Minoan art and religion.
Sometimes chthonic deity –
earth goddess
who curled, coiled herself
in matriarchy where the feminine
had a voice and creative power.

Divine Snake Goddess
Your eyes glint in mystic wisdom.
Truth flicks from your forked tongue.
You remind us of the divine feminine.
You remind us of the possible.

Your place setting, in earthy colours
of ivory and gold is decorated
with yellow accents in snake motifs.
The ceramic plate rooted in vulva imagery –
its four egg-shaped arms
power your generative force
as goddess.
Welcome to our dinner party.

Sophia

'And when you laid down the foundations of the earth, I was by your side, a unique craftswoman.' – Proverbs 8:22–31

Sophia is Goddess of Wisdom
apparelled in celestial light
honoured queen of the universe –
moon, sun, planets and stars.

From the time the mountains sang
and the rivers clapped hands
Sophia stood with the glory of the moon
intuitive, feminine.

Her prestige and fullness of life
trailed silver, lighting our path
through the dark ocean of history.

Her name, shared across cultures
as Athena, Inanna, Guan Yin, Tara
glows synergy in the heart of everywoman
in unity with the ruach of creation.

Michelangelo painted her as birther of creation.
'All life is created out of the Mother and is one with her'
affirmed mystics, seers and prophets centuries later.

It is hard to pinpoint the pivot
when this power was diminished
by patriarchy's wilful effort
when she was muted
seen as abstract, a token
constricted as an allegory.

Hagia Sophia, your dinner plate
with slender wands of petals unfolding
evokes you as supreme flower of light.*
Its deep centre and focal point
recalls your creative force –
the one who knows the world as a lover.

Yet your sacramental running cloth
covered with chiffon netting
pales – a veil of meekness
for the feminine
thwarted by societal power.
Sophia, singer of creation.
Welcome to our dinner party.

* from Sophia's *Song of Delight*

Amazon

Amidst the battle to affirm women
throughout history
Amazon women
with fierce inner conviction
self-possessed and resolute –
who donned breastplates
even prepared to cut off a breast
to be better archers
were warrior women
stalwart as Mars in the night sky
fiery red and untouchable
always with an extra stone for the sling
an extra arrow for the quiver.

Forged in the cauldrons of war
unified communities of women
trained in spear, battleaxe, lance
bow and arrow
fearsome as wild she-wolves
shielding cubs
they lost and won battles
feminine spirit blazing.

Ignored by military history
except in random footnotes
and erased from memory
except in Homer's telling
where the story
of unfettered female power
upheld gender equality.

Amazon Woman you strengthen
our resolve, give us pride in our sex.
Your place setting befits you –
the runner using imagery
of white egg, red crescent, black stone
reminds us of our power
in the rhythm of earth:
the double-headed axes
with breastplates in silver and gold
echo in your dinner plate
triangles allude to sacred feminine
and you as goddess.
Amazon Woman you are in everywoman.
Welcome to our dinner party.

Hatshepsut

'I am diademed with the red crown, I rule over this Egyptian land
like a son of Isis. I shall be forever the star which changeth not.'

In a new glorious age she walked
in the imperial garden
her show of roses flourished
as did her power and prosperity.

Hatshepsut was first Queen
elevated beyond the heavens
in the holy of holies
known to wear male attire
a beard, and nail polish
claiming 'His majesty herself.'

As Pharaoh she walked
in hand with the gods
revered in her temples
with reverence befitting a queen
in the Valley of Kings.

Her rule as constant as the Nile's flow
her command firm as the mountains
and she wooed the masses with generosity
in all twenty years of her peaceful reign.

Her sun-disk shimmered
its halo of honour – her female authority
falcon-high above her banner.

Yet Thuthmose II her successor
denied his lineage
being descended from a female pharaoh
erasing her name.

Hatshephut, Daughter of Re
you are not lost from our history.
We honour you the first woman
in recorded history to rule a nation.

Your Egyptian place setting
with hieroglyphic symbols
praising your reign
are embroidered
on fine Egyptian linen.
Your plate with menes-head cloth
of a Pharaoh
abides with us.
We lift our golden chalices
to your inspiration and presence.
Welcome to our dinner party.

Judith

'The Lord will deliver Israel by my hand.' – Judith, 8.23

Out of the darkness of fear
Judith, a widowed Hebrew woman
emerged with the glow
of a dawning.

Her walled city besieged.
Her blanched leaders, impotent
with terror, plan a surrender
to the enemy, certain death
to her people.

Judith prayed and fasted.
The voice of courage sang to her
declaring 'a woman will save Jerusalem
the Temple and the Israelite people!'
The paralysed magistrates
draped in despair
buckled to her commands.

She removed her mourning garb
bathed, perfumed
a festive dress, sandals, tiara
adorned her allure –
neck, arms, ankles with glint of jewels.

With armour of beauty and faith
Judith and her maid left the city
to confront the Assyrians
plunderers who had massacred
all in their wake, bent on
world domination.

With cunning and daring
she seduced the leader Holofernes.
Beguiled by her beauty
he was trapped. In a drunken
fumble to rape and conquer
he was beheaded,
in his own tent
with his own sword,
surrounded by his own hubristic army.

Artists, poets, musicians colour the myth
with seduction, blood, murder –
how evil was defeated at the hand of a woman
how chastity overcame lust
how Judith, a Hebrew woman
returned triumphant
and how at the sight
of Holoferne's severed head
the enemy fled.

Judith, saviour of your people
deemed helpless, dismissed by men
you learnt to take power.
Your wisdom used male assumptions
to your advantage.
The dramatic play of light and dark
of your place setting speaks to this enigma.
Welcome to our dinner party.

Sappho

'Someone…will remember us in time to come.' – Fragment 147

Across the blue Aegean sea
Sappho, weaver of words
sings down the centuries.

Astride a rocky acropolis
on her Greek Isle of Lesbos
she calls on her muses
Aphrodite, Eros
…burning…burning
a slender fire under her skin.

From the haven of her island
redolent with grain, grapes, olive groves
she is the dawn, arms like roses
her song aflame
with desire and yearning.

She ignored the epic poems
shunned praise for warriors and war.

In a time when men were the artists
intellects and leaders
Sappho wrote the language of sex
erotic passion, songs
with colour and texture.
Her lambent light stole hearts.
Green envy, jealous words
cleaved senses as wind
bends mountain oaks.

How to love a woman –
Sappho wrote,
'far more sweet-sounding then a lyre
more golden than gold.'
With sweet-bitter intimacy
of love and longing
she set her words to music
twining metre and sensual artistry.

Deliberately, her oeuvre
was lost to history, smothered
by male domination, ignorantly
consigned to a rubbish pit.

A millennium on
with delicate brushstrokes
scholars scrambled to piece together
papyrus fragments to satiate our hunger.
Her every word an aphrodisiac
she stirred ambiguity and curiosity
only to be destroyed again
by 4th century Church authority.

Sappho, you give us your ecstatic songs.
Called 'the flower of graces'
you are immortalised
on ancient urns and reliefs.
Plato acknowledged you —
poetess…tenth muse.

Your floral place setting
is glazed in lavender and emerald petals
with flourish of vulva motif.
Your runner, outlined
with hieroglyphics, embroidered
in wavy eruptions of colour
and hint of long flowing hair
bursts with female creativity.
Welcome to our dinner party.

Aspasia of Miletus

'Aspasia…a female Socrates.' – Cicero

When the curtain opened
on a classic golden age
with its burgeon of critical thought
a young girl, Aspasia, alert and curious
was schooled by her father
and despite Athenian law
refused to be ignored.

When she realised her father's name
was documented as were her sons
she spurned her anonymity.

She enhanced her name as a woman –
listened to for her eloquence
admired for her pedagogy
and her slant on philosophy.

Socrates, alert to her style of rhetoric
acclaimed her his muse.
His scholars gathered at her salon
some bringing their wives
to listen to her discourse.
She influenced Plato to welcome
the first women into his academy.
Pericles saw the beauty of her mind
beyond her flowing auburn hair
and as his romantic partner
her heartfelt, holistic spirit
guided his speeches –
moulding Imperial Greece.

When the curtain fell
on the century's glory
patriarchal storms raged.
In the cruel burst of Western thought
Aspasia was belittled, undermined
amidst jest and taunts of 'harlot'
her gathering of scholars
defamed as a brothel
her name erased
from the array of wisdom figures
shouldering early Western thought.

Aspasia, we applaud you
and marvel as we awaken
to your influence
in earlyWestern thought.
Your place setting –
ceramic floral patterns
blossomed in Greek motifs
and on fabric, gathered as a chiton.*
We imagine you in white toga, draped
and jewel-clasped
to illuminate your place in history's theatre.
Welcome to our dinner party.

* A chiton is a greek toga draped and fastened by clasp.

Boadaceia

When they heard how her rallying cries
unified the dispirited tribes
to rise to defend Britons' isle
from Roman lust and manic power...

when they knew the druids spurred her on
upon their knees in sacred groves
under giant oaks in spilt blood
their gods divining her rightful rebellion...

when they saw her, straight of stature
tawny red hair flying
her brown mantle fastened by a golden brooch
riding a chariot to victory...

they honoured her – their warrior,
'Briton queen'
bleeding from the Roman rods
vengeance in her eyes, spear in hand
full of rage, full of grief.

Yet Boadaceia, through history
you were ridiculed
called a shameless harridan
mocked in theatre
by those who could not fathom
a woman, a pagan as their saviour.
It took another woman – Queen Victoria
a thousand years on, to honour you.

We proclaim your warrior status
with your place setting.
Its curvilinear forms speak
to your valour, female strength.
Your dinner plate –
a stylised ceramic golden helmet
adorned in Celtic patterns
is a tribute to your roots.
Welcome to our dinner party.

Hypatia

Under her father's tutelage
her young eyes scanned
the spangled velvet sky
converted measurable patterns
into brilliant mathematical predictions.
As a woman wrapped in philosopher's cloak
her knowledge found a wider horizon
in astronomy and mathematics.
She held her scrolls high
as batons to be passed.
In the Alexandria agora
her students listened, respected her.

Angrily dismissed by Roman clerics
seen as a threat to the Church's teaching
scorned a soothsayer
her knowledge – witchcraft.
Her vicious murder left a trail of blood
on the cobbles –
no thunderous rain could wash away.

Hypatia, you are acclaimed
the world's first woman astronomer.
You sit at our table with classic Greek pride.

Your vibrant place setting with leaf motifs
of Coptic tapestries notes your courage.
Your beauty enhanced
with woven bands of wool
mouth masked in black tape
encircled by embroidered weeping
female images.
A moulded butterfly bursts
from the ceramic dinner plate
its scalloped edges a tribute
to your confidence.
It wings above cleric constraints.
Your voice threatened
their patriarchy.
Welcome to our dinner party.

Wing Two
Beginnings of Christianity to the Reformation

'We cannot live in a world that is not our own, in a world that is interpreted for us by others. An interpreted world is not a home. Part of the terror is to take back our own listening, to use our own voice, to see our own light.'
– Hildegard of Bingen

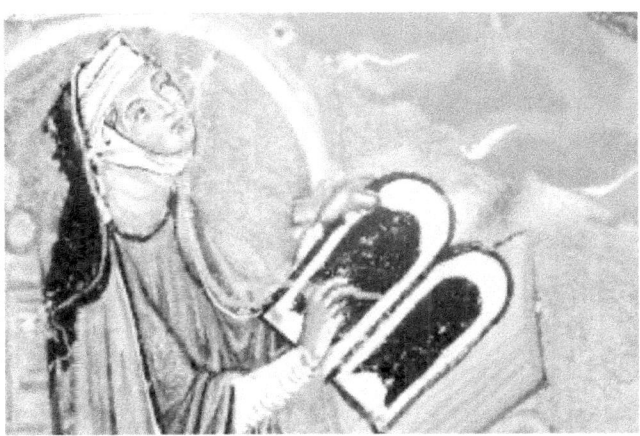

Marcella of Rome

A noble woman
caught in the cross beams
of love and light of God.
Marcella listened to the Word
relinquished wealth
made her home
an ark of refuge –
a fledgling cloister.
She gave young women an alternative
to betrothal and childbirth
as they exchanged their worldly
brocaded robes for brown
camel and hessian garments.

Convent life flowered –
a commune with beatitude
artisans, scribes, healers
keeping house and gardens
nourished and sustained
by ascetic learning and prayer.

A learned woman
Marcella was equal in scholarship
to St Jerome.
He tells us he dared not speak
of her intellect to other men
lest they be threatened.

And some were threatened –
soldiers in ignorance and anger
caused the women to flee
ransacked the convent,
beating Marcella to death.

And like so many women of her time
she was rubbed from history.

Marcella we revive your memory
and honour you
a pathfinder for women
a bridge between two worlds.
You connected with the Goddess
you connected with the Christ.
By praying in the *orans* posture
you challenged the male-only tradition
of this priestly *mudra*.
You chose to be empowered
before women were visible.
The first woman to sit
on this wing of our table.
Welcome to our dinner party.

Bridget

From the mists of time
Goddess by ten thousand names
Bridget was the echoing well
coming in the morning dew
her verdancy
the dawn of Imbolc.
Her healing balm enfolded all
from cold hibernation.
The daughter of the winter sun
edging springtime in collusion
with green leaves and oak trees.
Ripe with all seasons
she was the flame
in the furnace of transformation.

Enter Bridget, young fiery Christian
kindled from the goddess
glowing with the passion of youth.
Saint and virgin, she gathers
a following of women
to work, pray, give their life to God
inspiring convents
across homeland and beyond.

Ireland's goddess saint, Bridget
draws in the light
the way a morning glory opens
to the sun after the dark of night.

A hearthstone of welcome
burning with Druid devotion
always her life enflamed with fervour.

Bridget, your place setting
edged with Celtic knots
carved in your *muiredach* cross
speaks of unity with audacity.
Your ceramic plate –
rich red, blue and Irish green
extols your presence with us.
Welcome to our dinner party.

Theodora

'Are we not straitly bound to prosecute the robbers of honour and the thieves of chastity?'

Theatre calls for colour, drama.
Enter with flare onto her first stage
Theodora, born into a circus family.
Draped in garlands from a young age
entertainer of crowds
star of Constantinople's hippodrome.

Dressed as a concubine
a sensual dancer
seductress
salacious in the role of *Leda and the Swan*.

When mistreated and abandoned
she found a tenacity to transcend –
bravely acted, improvised, endured
soothed her way into the Byzantine court.

Was she a dancer, when Justin's eye
fell on her beauty, a love that overcame
all barriers?

Theodora emerged an actor
on a new Imperial stage –
Empress of the Eastern World.

Mosaic murals show Theodora
seated with her Emperor –
partnership, equality, respect.
Under their leadership
the ancient world vibrated with life.

Facing plague, betrayal, riots,
Theodora wooed back
the trust of their people
to grasp a new vision –
to fashion a better world.
During their reign, Constantinople
grew into a glorious city –
Hagia Sophia, jewel of the Byzantine crown.

Theodora defied patriarchy and misogyny.
Her pressure for marriage and property laws
gave women dignity and new rights
demanded that men view them
more as human beings!

She banned pimps, saved girls sold
into sexual slavery
giving women of her time
their choice of destiny.

Theodora, you gave your life
to elevate the place of women.
We claim you an avant-garde feminist.

Your place setting has mosaic
tiles of gold, green and purple
with an abstract butterfly.
Each wing stretching to the plate's edge
reminds us how you created freedoms
with your indomitable spirit.
Welcome to our dinner party.

Hrosvitha

Hrosvitha fired up the cauldron
of tenth century Saxony
forging a new way –
a vow of chastity and life in an abbey.

Smouldering against the world
her alchemy of choice
meant freedom, independence –
empowering her
to become the first woman writer
of the Germanic world.

Her story is engraved
into Saxony woodcuts –
queen of medieval theatre
at the centre of a literary world
poet, playwright, priestess
with a great style in wimples!

Intimacy held her infatuated
even as she blushed.
She knew the wild heart
of woman beating within.
It tantalised her stories of love
as she chose to celebrate
love in women
in contrast to the Roman plays
of debauchery and lust.

Hrosvitha, you are our link
giving women a voice
even though your voice
would be engulfed
in the fire of patriarchy.
Like steel from the furnace
your link would never be broken.

Your place setting
has embroidered roundels
heralding a privileged position
untouchable for negators.
Your ceramic plate features
a carved nun's cap
and hands clasped in prayer
in humble tones of ivory.
Welcome to our dinner party.

Trota of Salerno

Trota, a woman physician
played her cards well.
She was fortunate to be born
into a time of renaissance
and into an educated family
in Salerno then crossroads
of Byzantine and Western thought
with its famous International
Medical Academy.

When most relied on
relics and prayer in sickness
Trota gave us women's health care.
She scribed her scientific research
with Latin-labelled anatomy drawings.
Yet her study and medical manuscripts
were appropriated by men
and claimed impossible to come
from the mind of a woman!

She rose out of a medieval canvass
wracked by dark times, fear
and bible-black stains of superstition
then was lost to history for 900 years.

Visualise her, charismatic
tall, stoic, white-veiled
in green flowing gown
red cloak
a golden orb held high.

Hear her
demand the use of opiates
in childbirth
defy the taboo that women must suffer
because of Eve's sin!

When she died, mourners
led a procession two miles long,
claiming *magistra mulier sapiens**
yet by the 13th century
women were again excluded from university.
Her writings unnamed, masked, absorbed.

Trota, we reclaim your presence.
What history smothered, we return.
Your place setting features
images of birthing with background
of the medicinal motif 'tree of life'
Your dinner plate with the *Staff of Hermes*
honours you –
Professor of Medicine.
Welcome to our dinner party.

---

* *magistra mulier sapiens*: wise woman teacher

Eleanor of Aquitaine

Out of the darkness of gendered history
comes a young girl
a fragile flower growing from rocky ground –
empathy capturing her heart
like sunlight.

Eleanor of Aquitaine
wearing a crown of morning air
illuminated her Renaissance world
inspired the arts and culture
a time of courtly love and chivalry.

Picture her face flowering
with defiance against conventions,
seated straight-backed on her horse
golden hair flowing with the wind
gowned in silk, cerise-red
gold thread and fine fur-lined cloak
fastened with jewelled pins.

She became to poets
what dawn is to birds.
Minstrels sang salutations
to her beauty.
Along pilgrim routes
troubadours and balladeers
carried her in their song.

Picture her in fullest bloom defying
conventions as first Queen of France
then with crown of English roses.
As mother of kings
Eleanor transcended
a world dominated by men.

Imagine her feeling of betrayal
when King Louis claimed
annulment, for lack of a son;
when King Henry imprisoned her
within cold walls.

After sixteen years of his denial
Eleanor ruled as capably as any man –
Queen in her own right
paragon among women.

When anxiety and stress
became her companions
vulnerable and alone
she took refuge in a French abbey
where life wilted like petals
from a fallen flower.

'Eleanor passed from the world
as a candle in the sconce goeth out
when the wind striketh it.'

Eleanor, your place setting
features the mystical unicorn
imprisoned by corrals in
middle age tapestries
with fleur-de-lis design
symbol of Mary, Queen of Heaven
her gown deep blue for fidelity with
blades of grass, symbol of a heart
pierced by sorrow.

Like a comet
you trail across the centuries
brightening a dark story.
You hold a dazzling light to women's history.
Welcome to our dinner party.

Hildegard of Bingen

'O greening branch! You stand in your nobility like the rising dawn.'

Hildegard of Bingen lived the blue skies
flowers, feathers, herbs, bees and gems
to heal, to soothe and calm:
the canvas of her life radiant with colour
bursting with aliveness.

The hierarchy of the Church
strove to silence her.
She confronted patriarchy
ignorance, superstition, fear, betrayal.
From this darkness and pain
Hildegard spoke. She composed
and sang and wrote.
She travelled and preached.

She led her sisters
to build their own abbey
gave jubilance with her music.
She built. In pockets of stillness
with three pillars –
prayer, work and study
shawled by cerulean hills
and the song of the Rhine.

A Renaissance woman
she found belief in herself –
with opposition
from the Church's hierarchy
she strove to live deliberately
stood steadfast
resolute in Spirit
for herself
for all women.
'it is not in the power
of an armed man to seize you'
she wrote in song.

A cosmic woman
with deep reverence for mother earth
she warned,
'The earth sustains humanity,
it must not be injured; it must not be destroyed.'

Hers was a healing world,
with the blessing of *viriditas**
like grass upon which dew falls
– a thousand shades of green
and what is this but hope?

---

* *viriditas* is the union of two Latin words: green and truth, coined by Hildegard of Bingen.

Hildegard, silenced, suppressed
by her Church,
lost to history for 800 years
is found today by musicians, poets, artists
environmentalists, herbalists and healers.
All bask in her glow
fuelled by the fire and passion
that burned within her.

Hildegard, our foremother
you are a touchstone for women's history.
Your place setting, a tribute
to your sagacity.
The ceramic and stained glass
dinner plate set in an embroidered arch
of a gothic cathedral
and your place setting
with its cosmic illumination
lifts our vision beyond the horizon.

How fitting – you are seated
in the middle of the ages
a pivot between eras amongst women

When we listen, your celestial music
a *Te Deum* for our spirit still sings.
Welcome to our dinner party.

Petronilla de Meath

In the marketplace
they are piling sticks
building stakes
to fuel a fire
that will enflame the world.

Whispers of heresy
jolt women, midwives and healers
who were sought out
in times of sickness and childbirth
for their folk wisdom
who garnered plants, herbs and stones
intuited salves, balms
distilled the healing powers of the earth

While her mistress travelled
gossip accused Petronilla –
a young apprentice
with whispers of magic, black cats
broom sticks and spell potions.

Dragged from parish to parish
whipped, tortured
to satisfy the bishop's anger
to incite the mob
eager for the smell of heretic flesh
to satisfy the Papal Inquisition
Petronilla a healer is burnt at the stake.

Caught in a crucible of pagan belief
blazing superstition and intolerance
a burning page of cruelty begins.

It will take a rebellion of women to rise
phoenix-like over the next centuries
for this abscess that festered
at dark age of history to be excised.

Petronilla, you are the first gallant woman
lost in the garb of fiery light
flames used by church leaders
to destroy female power
fearful of women's intuition.

Your ceramic plate
is forged from the sacred fire that triumphs
and burns for the Goddess.
Your runner with
its embroidered cauldron,
fires the womb in us all –
alchemy for our sisters.
It is an honour to share your presence.
Welcome to our dinner party.

Christine de Pizan

'The same race as men are women. It is a woman's world too.'

Crow quills, pigments and ink
parchment, vellum, Parisian scribes –
were Christine de Pizan's world.

In French Medieval Courts
encircled by books and learning
her pen forged her independence.

Her writings, copied and shared
validated women's self-worth
broke open locked chambers
of possibility
– 'bestsellers' of her day,

With books, poems – ballads of courtly love
Christine took on misogynists
lined up their arguments and obscenities
knocking them down
like rigid cold tenpins
one by one
with her battering logic.

Christine dared to defend
women's rights to education
affirmed their skills
and contributions to the world.

She wrote of 'a world' where great women
were silenced.
Recent trawls of history
have re-netted her words
rescued her from the ocean of darkness –
one who visualised a society
that valued equality

You, Christine de Pizan inspired
women authors of the Renaissance
in an age when a woman's voice was silenced
and independence near impossible.
Your gift of knowledge and feminism
offered to the medieval world
is a gift to all women.

Here your plate, like a butterfly
with one wing raised in a gesture of defiance
endorses your work as champion of women.
Welcome to our dinner party.

Isabella d'Este

Into an expanding world
whirl of wealth and education
is born a dynamic woman –
Isabella d'Este.
A generous patron of the arts
collector of antique articles
she spurred a swelling
of Italian Renaissance.

An intrepid intellectual
mother of seven children
she made girls' education her forte.

When her husband, Marquis of Mantua
was taken hostage
her leadership proved stellar
in negotiating his freedom
stabilising a peace.

As Marchioness of Mantua
she eclipsed her husband and son
established herself
as a First Lady in Europe.
She led her people out of war
through plague and dire famine
refused to be smothered by history
and through her correspondence
gives us a window
into her generation.

Isabella sought the best limners of her day –
Leonardo sketched her as a mona lisa
a Titian portrait belied her sixty years.
Her city, Mantua, matured
as a centre of culture –
its innovative fashion
copied, throughout Italy and France.

We can imagine you
at your courts
in jewel-studded Titian gown
admired by your protégés –
painters, musicians, writers, scholars
as a *trouvère** of Virgil's poetry.

Your place setting highlights
Renaissance –
perspective, horizon, vanishing points.
The runner is designed with tassels, shields
and the decorative fleur-de-lys
reserved for the nobility of your time.
Welcome to our dinner party.

---

* *trouvere*: a medieval epic poem, northern France, 11th–14th century

Regina, Elizabeth I

'I have the heart and stomach of a king.' Elizabeth R

Amid storms of court intrigue
religious terrorism, death
and dangerous dismay
a young woman entered London.
Amid bells and bonfires
in a grand coronation
she was crowned Virgin Rose Elizabeth R

How radiantly she bloomed
how bold and freely she flowered
ruling her empire with Tudor iron
denying sorcerers and dragons
muting soothsayers
she weaved her cabal web.
How her flirtatious affairs
myth and reality of love and lust
intrigued Europe's halls of gossip.

In England she ripped great holes
in the injustice of witch trials
demanded better treatment of women
spoke out for equity in the courts.

Fearless in a golden age of expansion
she lead her peerless Royal Navy
with Amazonian resolution
steel cuirass over her white velvet gown.
On a white gelding in plumed helmet
gold truncheon in hand
she bequeathed hope to her people.

Steadily she *became* her portraits
hundreds of portraits, hundreds of gowns –
golden, glorious, embroidered
wide hooped with boned kirtles.
Breast plated in gold
pearl beads and rhinestone
she was manifested untouchable –
beyond human.

A prisoner in her own life
in time she paced walled cloisters
a 'Helen of Troy' in her palace
tethered to her chamber
to a bedroom
to a death bed.
As petals fall the rose wilts.

Queen Regina, your place setting
of regal blue and gold
with rich crimson
speaks of your royalty.
We claim you, erudite woman
of the sixteenth century
powerful, monumental yet
amid the glamour, lonely.
Welcome to our dinner party.

Artemisia Gentileschi

'I have the spirit of Caesar and the soul of a woman.'

In her hands
the brush swept the canvass
azure blue, old gold, crimson red.

At her rape trial, Artemisia
under torture of thumb-screws
never quailed.
Her only fear was for her artist hands
as her voice screamed her truth
veritas, veritas, it is true, it is true.

It is these abused hands
that turned the horror of life into art.
A war cry for oppressed women of her time
a Baroque prescience of women's advocacy.

It is these tormented hands
that painted the sword that Judith holds
that heaves and plunges
beheading Holofernes
as a woman saving her people.

Artemisia, in her paintings
rebuffed the book of rules
and cultural norms
reinterpreted biblical and mythical stories
so well ensconced to hold up patriarchy –
revisioned stories where men painted women
seducers, whores, coy, meek, weak.
She painted them strong.
Her self-portraits emboldened,
embodied with sleeves rolled up
exposed her muscular forearms
and those large powerful hands.

She was liberated by disgrace
paid her bills in paint and flesh
summoning sensuality in her
nudes with play of light.

In life and in art she showed
more than any man, the way
a woman's flesh settles and softens.

When academic doors
were closed to women
she fought and finally found success
acclaimed and given patronage
Then lost to history for 400 years.

Artemisia, we reclaim you
revolutionary woman artist.
Your ceramic plate twists and turns
a butterfly effect of light and shadow.
We are reminded of your illumination
in the darkness of your time.

Artemisia, you leap from your world
with blazing realism, to be our contemporary.
As you cried out at your trial,
'I will show you what women can do'
We see you today and acclaim you.
Welcome to our dinner party

Anna Maria van Schurman

'Woman has the same wish for self-development as man, the same ideals, yet she is to be imprisoned in an empty soul of which the very windows are shuttered.'

Anna Maria, scaled walls of her day
no biased confinement for her
language skills her ladder
to new vistas and marvellous
worlds of possibility.
Each rung braced correspondence
with strong women all over Europe.
Her treatises on woman's right to education
poured new wine into the old skins of conformity.

Even when the skin cracked and wine like blood spilled
the new idea of 'woman as a human' stained like old logic.
She endorsed the radical agendas
of visionaries – Galileo, Bacon, Newton
who challenged foundations of knowledge
but even they always halted –
halted at the portal of gender.

She not only pried this door open
she jammed her foot in it
giving oxygen to a suffocating time –
when women were still excluded from university
when girls were deprived of formal education
when it was thought the female sex
did not have aptitude for study.
Her acknowledgement of women
blazed light into writings
about humanity.

As first woman to go to a Dutch University
she heralded a new dawn
even though relegated to sit in a veiled closet
so as not to disturb the male students!

Her Dissertation on the Education of Women
her discussions with Descartes on logic
meant the door was no longer closed
albeit with centuries of struggle ahead.

The last woman of the Middle Ages at our table –
you impugned the darkness for women
repositioned them in the struggle.
Anna van Schurman
we are indebted to your fervour
to your celibate life
and your wisdom that shone
into the dark corners of your time.

At our dinner party, your plate –
an abstract orange butterfly
etched with fine lines as if eager to be free
symbolises your polymathic thinking
your valiant efforts for women's rights.
The runner embroidered
in 17th century Dutch style
reminds us of swatch-like patches
young girls sewed
to teach them docility, obedience
and to 'think small'
Welcome to our dinner party.

Wing Three
Beginnings of the
Women's Revolution

'If society will not admit of woman's free development
then society must be remodelled.'
– Elizabeth Blackwell

Anne Hutchinson

'I will stand the ground for what I know to be true.'

Winter wind howled
slapped rigid blows against the window.
Courtroom draughts shuddered
driven by a New England freeze
while insulated by purity of faith
a whorl of forty black-garbed
judges of piety and learning
circled the stand.

At the still point
a woman stood
her right hand pointed upwards.
Her voice, acute and defiant
belied her small stature. Strands of hair
fell from under her white bonnet
onto her determined brow.
A cloak of black wool swathed her pregnancy
as she parried charges of heresy and sedition.

As midwife and healer, her assertion
'a woman's body is not up for religious debate'
swept her further into turmoil.
With fearless biblical rhetoric
she testified her right to preach –
the judges, inadequate to foil
her shrewd intellect.

After two long-drawn-out trials
Anne Hutchinson heard the verdict –
banishment
for 'behaving in a manner not fitting your sex.'
Sent out in the winter of 1638
to walk in thigh-deep snow
she bore her stillborn child
Judge Winthrop's words flailing in her ears
'this American Jezebel
a new Eve, enemy of the chosen'.

The air was stiff with patriarchy
misogyny an acrid stench.
No zephyr of compromise.
Yet her violent death in exile –
could not quash her legacy.

History disdained her as arrogant
fanatical, rebellious.
It took three hundred years
to be claimed as 'a founding mother
a suffragist before suffragists'
by Eleanor Roosevelt –
another forty years
before a formal pardon.

Anne, there is a touch of lament
at your place setting –
with its embroidered shawl worn
by women in grief, reflecting
this low point
in the history of women.
Muted earth tones speak
of mourning for the struggle
women still face.
Today we rejoice in your life
celebrate your vision and courage.
Welcome to our dinner party.

Sacajawea

'I was taken in the middle of the river as I was crossing at a shallow place to make my escape.'

It was a journey, such a long journey
the ways deep, weather sharp
arid plains, wild rivers, hostile tribes –
the trail west across America's unknown.

Sacajawea, a barefoot Shoshone girl
shiny black plaited hair
a baby son wrapped in deerskin
papoosed on her back –
smoothed the way
as guide and interpreter
across the labyrinthine Rockies.

Her dexterity with a canoe
ability to bargain for horses
her innate knowledge
of earth's bountiful medicines, foods
and star navigation, meant survival –
success for Lewis and Clark's
famous expedition west.

We only know of Sacajawea from journals –
'our squaw is handy with her knife
she cuts wood, meat and fish
splits rushes for mats and baskets
fashions skins for clothes and moccasins.'
and that she was beaten often
by a polygamist husband
as nothing more than his bibelot.

Upon return she went unsung
in myth and memory –
isolated from her destiny
distanced from her story
stolen, sold and enslaved
and for a century, forgotten.
History has restored her
a most courageous woman
emblem of tenacity and power.

Sacajawea, we reclaim you.
Quiet heroism
is your silence. Only your actions
reveal your thoughts –
your mythical worth deemed
more important than your race.
Here a proud Native American place setting
with its runner of hand-tanned deerskins
edged with opaque wild seed beads.
Your ceramic plate in chestnut and teal
speaks strongly of your bravery.
Welcome to our dinner party.

Caroline Herschel

'What we see, we see and seeing is changing' – Adrienne Rich

A father's warm hand
a frosty night, shimmering skies
shared elation at a comet.
Its cold white light, fires
a young girl's imagination.

Destined for servitude as housemaid
with cleaning jobs in store
Caroline's life teeters.
Her brother rescues her
Cinderella-like
into a happy-ever-after life.

As an amateur astronomer
he makes her his housekeeper –
lens polishing by day, scrutinising
the heavens and notation by night!

Even in drifting snows
Caroline was there
a small shawled figure
perched on a large telescope frame
forever sweeping the skies.
Enchantment of night sky mystery
overcame the cold, lonely darkness.

With backbone of perseverance
she flung open constellations of possibility
for women and science –
observed, recorded, calculated, mapped
until the very ink froze on her quill.

Caroline, discoverer of eight comets
was known only as William's sister.
The Royal Astronomical Society refused her
entry, even to read her research.

Caroline, you proved yourself –
persevered until you gained
the Society medal in 1835.
At ninety-six years old
honoured by your homeland
with Prussia's Gold Medal of Science
pioneer astronomer, a path-maker –
your life's work notable before your time.

At your place setting, needlework
embroiders a sweep of the cosmos
clouds and stars cradle your comets.
Your ceramic place with its internal eye
honours your faithfulness
focus and fidelity.
Welcome to our dinner party.

Mary Wollstonecraft

'I do not wish women to have power over men; but over themselves.'

Sharp oaky smell of ink
dip and scratch of nib
Mary inhales the air
sits back in her leather chair
her desk a mosaic of papers.

She has come to feel at home –
as writer, editor, reviewer
a voice within the
radical groups of London
hears accolades for her treatise
with its strident call for girls to be educated
affirmed to speak out
ignite a feminist consciousness.
'to make women better mothers'

She sees herself a modern kind of being –
first of a new genus
forging a revolution for her sex.

'I can no longer tread this beaten track'
she writes to her sister.
'Women must have opportunity to develop
their own reason. The world can only flourish
among equals.'

Her voice was a luminous candle
in a darkness of patriarchy
where laws claimed women
the property of men
marriage their tenuous security.
This spirited her struggle
her weapon always her pen.

A passionate visionary
with her expansionist thinking and writing
for her two daughters and all women
she fiercely coveted more.

Little could she know her light
would flicker out
with death in childbirth.
Little could she know revelation
of her unorthodox lifestyle
would eclipse
her enlightened sagacity.
Little could she know its controversy
would smother her work for a century.

Mary, we claim you, mother of feminism.
You shifted the ground
challenged men's claim to their certainty.
Your ceramic plate
three-dimensional, strong and assertive
embodies your will and intelligence.
Your runner of meticulous needlework
shows scenes of your gendered confines
and rawly, your difficult and painful childbirth.
Your calamitous life cut short
epitomises women's story through history.
We stand in awe at what you did
for the advancement of women
in your short years.
Welcome to our dinner party.

Sojourner Truth

'Lord, I have done my duty, I have told the whole truth and kept nothing back.'

A battlefield thunders
through her heart
in the midst of an Ohio convention.
She stands tall
broad as a man baring her breasts.
Fierceness fires her belly.
In a deep imposing voice
with its thick Dutch accent
her words
'Ain't I a woman?'
ran like blood through the veins of the country
through the veins of history –
a challenge to racial and gender equality.

Sojourner, a young black woman
born into bondage
a girl ripped from her mother
bought and sold as a slave
whipped and abused
carried her scars as her secret.
Even her mangled slave hand
is hidden by yarns of wool
in the only known photo.

Seeds of faith – her compass
to escape slavery –
lift her above the battlement of fear.
Fierce love knows no barrier.
Freedom flows into a distant star
shaping an improbable landscape.
Her perspective, an endless horizon.

Sojourner Truth – prophetess,
travelling preacher
you arrived with your wicker bag
at booked churches and halls
where your voice raised the rafters.
People crowded to hear your eloquence.
A red carpet of reputation
spread before you.

At your place setting we validate you.
Janus symbol features on your ceramic plate –
a tear-faced girl shadowed by a woman
with raised fist, two faces, two breasts
in blatant defiance of church wardens –
men, demanding proof that you are woman
men, denying that one who exhibits your power
could be the phenomenal woman you are.
Phenomenal woman,
welcome to our dinner party.

Susan B. Anthony

'Women will not be taken seriously till they can vote.'

And so, as a young woman
in the flush of life, she ensnared herself
into the briar and bias of her time
determined not to be owned by any man.
She walked a pathless way
to find her inspiration.

To attend her first convention
she hurdled sexist norms –
and 'founding fathers' entitlement.
Rising proudly to speak
as chosen delegate
she was silenced –
'Women are here to listen and to learn.'

Such seeds were planted that day
as she stood and walked out
discovering she had followers
rich friendships in sisterhood
with strong emotional bonds
and a radical sense of purpose.

A suffragist movement was born.
Abolitionist and temperance groups
rallied – marches swelled.
With charisma, that demanded attention
her voice became a force.
Ridicule armed her – a woman of mettle.

Other passionate women
grouped around her.
With their collective wisdom and skills
they hammered out speeches
prepared petitions, papers, flyers
wrote suffragist history.

In her black, full-skirted gown
Susan scrambled onto a billiard tables
clutched megaphones, knocked
gavels outside men's meetings
and held speaking tours in packed halls.

'Are women persons?'
was her rally cry of protest.

In 1872, when against the law
she loudly caste a vote
she was arrested, tried, fined
condemned and ridiculed
in all the newspapers –
her voice energised by default
'we women are no longer a footnote'

'I thought the constitution began: We the people…
    not, We the white male citizens…
        the only question left to be settled now is:
            Are women persons?' – Susan Anthony

In your revolution to change thinking
Susan, you bit your lip – tasted the blood
of sacrifice. Your vibrant spirit never dimmed.
Your eyes gazed into the future –
inspiring all to continue…
'with women together, failure is impossible.'

Here at our dinner party
your place runner pins your vision
for voting rights for women
your fiery red plate, a symbol
of the struggle of a suffragette's life.
Susan you saw beyond the horizon
of the hope, not won in your lifetime.
Welcome to our dinner party.

Elizabeth Blackwell

'If society will not admit of woman's free development then society must be remodelled.'

A patriarchal fortress of belief
needed someone of courage
and persistence to penetrate
its barred portals.

Elizabeth Blackwell was such a one.
A plaque in her memory reads:
one who never turned her back
but marched, breast forward...

And this she did –
hungering to enter medical school
challenging a strictly male domain.
Undaunted by twenty-nine
jam-shut medical doors
her foot found a chink
into a small medical college.

Elizabeth endured four lonely years
to graduate the first woman doctor.

Fired by a reformist zeal
with the talons of an eagle
she pried open this forbidden world –
clawing back constant attempts
to stymie female doctors.

She inspired, taught
set up medical schools
fought stigmas, lingering superstitions
paced paths to hospitals
that refused female internships.

Your place setting Elizabeth
is a swirling scallop-edged plate
with an abstract butterfly effect.
The runner's rainbow colours
acclaim freedom that soared
out of a dark age.

We are grateful for your life's work
your triumphs amidst difficulties
in the field of medicine.
Your presence here honours us all.
Welcome to our dinner party.

Emily Dickinson

'You are alone in your rebellion, Miss Dickinson.'

Spools of light slant
through murmurs of cloud
hardened, cold…cold.
'Always Winter Afternoons.'

'I've ceded – I've stopped being Theirs.'

Living her life
was her greatest art.
Defying 19th century mores
outspoken, inflexible, lonely –
lonely…

ostracised by the words of the local editor
– 'women cannot create
the permanent treasures of literature'

and only seven poems –
retitled, altered without permission
published as 'Anon'.

Yet no gloom could dull her strength.
She defied the world with her pen
honed the words of her jewel-like mind.
A sharp-sighted observer
she tore apart
the puritanic fabric
radicalised her era
forever changed the landscape of literature.

Poems were her solace
for the eternity which surrounds us all.
She left the world
hundreds of them, handwritten
in her commingling way
bound into small books
many folded into small notes
passed to her 'sister'
for editing. Some playful,
some intimate and personal
full of longing and devotion.

Tending her herbarium
her passion for botany
enwreathed her with flowers and trees
that she grew, gathered, pressed –
garnering words for poems –
her interplay of beauty and loss.

Emily, your veneer
eccentric…recluse
confined you to your house,
later to your room
labelled you an enigma
yet you billowed with playfulness
fully alive.

A frilly pink lace ceramic plate
reminds us you were almost smothered
by Victorian life
yet you epitomised the glory of martyrs
who sing while they suffer.
Welcome to our dinner party.

Ethyl Mary Smyth

'I must fight for my music because I want women…not to go on hugging the shore afraid to put out to sea.'

In the long dark of discrimination
when females were regarded as inferior
the composer Ethyl Smyth flamed
a fragment of women's story
fearlessly forging her musical career.

She sought study abroad with Brahms
and in England claimed
the glow of limelight for her symphonies.
She fought to be judged on merit
and bore the gender slings and arrows
too feminine! too masculine!
a remarkable achievement – for a woman!

With a strident stance
dressed in tweeds, deerstalker and tie
unashamedly self centred and determined
and under the name E.M. Smyth
her music received acceptance.
performed in London and New York.

Friendship with Emmeline Pankhurst
brought a sharp turn of energy.
Ethyl had found a new fight
a musical fight for the right to vote.
She composed 'The March of Women' –
a world-wide battle cry for equality
at this turbulent time in women's history.

With disruptive protests
with her fighting women
Ethyl was gaoled.

Change sang
through dank stone
with the hour chill as steel.
Through her cell bars Ethyl Mary Smyth
beat time with Bacchic frenzy –
her baton, a toothbrush!

Below, two hundred gaoled women
many on hunger strike roared
her suffragette anthem –

> *Shout shout up with your song…*
> *March march swing you along.*

Her music their megaphone, their solace
their only succour.

Only now ninety years on
have you been reclaimed.
Your symphony, *The Prison*
is finally hailed, recorded
and your name now proudly
feminised – Ethyl Smyth.

In your place setting
we can hear music of assertiveness
with the dinner plate moulded as a grand piano.
Odd numbers of keys
speak of eccentricity.
The runner a cut of worsted, confined –
for the once containment
of an immense talent.
Welcome to our dinner party.

Margaret Sanger

'Every woman can decide for themselves.' (*Time* magazine, 1932)

Death and fear drive hard lessons.
Margaret knew her mother's death –
body spent after eighteen births;
and heartache, holding
her young friend's hand
dying from a botched self-abortion.

Nursing the underprivileged
she saw how unwanted pregnancies
caged womanhood.
How even when the gate slid ajar
many, in fear, stayed fettered.

She resolved to dedicate her life
to fight for birth control –
a human right to empower women.
She blazed with wrath
as she was censored, called loose, vulgar.
Her voice was silenced.
Her writings banned.

Arrested, charged, self-exiled for a time –
all gave eagle wings to her determination.
She proclaimed,
'enforced motherhood is the most complete denial
of a woman's right to life and liberty'.

Margaret showed how one woman can win –
against man-made laws that impede change
against religion's megaphonic voice.

She triumphed.
The shackles eased.
A new era of justice for women
was birthed yet the pangs endured.
Like a genie freed
there is no end…
her coined phrase 'birth control'
was and still is weaponised
accused of being eugenics.

Today, a woman must be ever vigilant.
The fight for right over her own body
never ends.

Margaret, today you hold
a vaunted place in history.
Your vision untethered
expansive as the horizon.

A blood-red burnished glaze
highlights your place setting.
Your plate, like the Sangria butterfly
– symbol of freedom –
captures the colour and spirit
of our womanhood.
Welcome to our dinner party.

Natalie Barney

'Destiny made us women at a time when the law of men is the only law that is recognised.'

Waves of history break
against a stark backdrop of war.
Enter Natalie Barney, poet and writer
who drank the elixir of modernism.

A young woman lured
by the avant-garde of Paris
its flourish of free expression
free love, where forests could be red
and haystacks blue.
Her life overflowed with colour and creativity
blossoming in the Belle Époque
with its *joie de vivre*.

At her Friday Salon
Natalie was host to writers and artisans –
where boundaries shifted, values challenged
old ways changed –
and her soirees afforded women
a cachet of equality.

Within the crests and troughs of her time
she created an inviolable space
L'Academie des Femmes
her answer to the citadel of the Male Academy.
Buoyed by her American childhood
she pursued her dreams
to free feminism from a destiny
that held women in chains;
where the only law was the law of men.

Her wild heart was to many lovers
'a page-boy of love sent by Sappho'
Her writings, defied
male bastions of control.

Natalie Barney, you pursued your dreams
shifting the canon for all women.

Your plate lustred in iridescent blue and violet
invokes your lavish Parisian life.
The art deco silk butterfly runner
symbolises the beat of wings – a lift off
to the world of new possibilities.
Welcome to our dinner party.

Virginia Woolf

'For most of history, Anonymous was a woman.'

The image of waves
incessant, recurrent, dip and crest
through Virginia Woolf's writing…
fluid writing, cyclical, repetitive
characters flowing into each other.

Like Arachne's woven web of story
her words spin, warp and weft
of stability below her hanging orb
of insecurity.

As rebellious as Arachne
to challenge history –
gendered history from a male perspective
Virginia must forge a new path
follow her instinct, her reason
find a new consciousness.

Liminality. She grasps
the spiral of holding experience
turning it over slowly in the light
making it real
finding for every wound
there is a word
a balm to soothe.

She writes to rhythm not to plot
her words liberate
with voices that sometimes crack.
Her veridity emanates from her circle –
free thought, free love.

Virginia your subversive spirit
and your feminism
infused with subtlety
opened up new possibilities.

Your Cambridge influence –
your writing and lectures
free us from shackles
of control. The feminist literary world
no longer stifled.

Your dinner plate bursts as a flower
from seeds of fecundity.
Because of you
'Anon' is a name of the past.
Welcome to our dinner party.

Georgia O'Keeffe

'The men liked to put me down as the best woman painter. I think I'm one of the best painters.'

She throws a large canvas
splashes it with colour
multicolour
cliffs and canyons vibrate with light
drops in a paradox –
a blue morning glory
delicate as a distant star
floats under the graceful twist
of a horn on the ram's skull –
a modern American *memento mori*
its bones, wind-sharp, keenly
alive with the sense of place.
The Santa Fe desert
vast, knowing no kindness
across its stark beauty.
'I was crazy about…the beauty of that wild world.'

A flamboyant obsessive artist,
Georgia O'Keeffe in severe black suits and Oxfords,
felt hat jammed on her black hair
found her rhythm
in the sweep of her environment.
Stripped to its essence
the landscape unlatched her heart.

In New Mexico, her *élan vita* flourished.
She painted her joy – flowers
clouds and sky, rocks and bones.
Her intense response to nature –
to capture the essence, the scent
of the sagebrush, the feel of the dusk.

Hers was a language of abstract form
of swirling intertwining flames and buds.
Yet a new feminine form
spurred anger in a male world.

Gender stereotypes
loomed like a hostile forest
to entangle her.
Through sickness, O'Keeffe –
despair with inner strength
prised a primal way.

Outraged by labels – sexual, sensual
belittling censure –
she demanded to be taken seriously.

Her stance marks the moment
women found new language.
From aloneness in the landscape
her inspiration was claimed
'pivotal in female iconography.'
She gave women new visibility.

Georgia O'Keefe, in your fierce struggle
for equality in the artist's world
you ensured strong shoulders
for future women to stand upon.
Harbinger of modernism
the most contemporary
at our table —
welcome to our dinner party.

Notes on the poems and women at the dinner party

Wing One

According to Thomas Berry, there is historical evidence of an earlier, more benign civilisation period, a matricentric period. From her studies, Judy Chicago concludes that 'all archaeological evidence indicates that these matriarchal cultures were egalitarian, democratic, peaceful. But female-oriented agricultural societies gradually gave way to a male-dominated political state in which occupational specialisation, commerce, social stratification, and militarism developed.'

A historical term for this time is prepatriarchy with special reference to the matricentric period which flourished from around 6500 BCE until the Aryan invasions around 3500 BCE. It was manifested in the goddess-centred religions.

From then through Western history we see the rise of patriarchy also now designated the patricentric period, which is coterminous with the Western civilisation process for the next five thousand years.

By using the suffix 'centric' rather than 'archal', we move from the idea of dominion or rule to that of cultural integrity.

Primordial Goddess, 6500 BCE

The original conception of the goddess is that of Mother Earth, the sacred female force responsible for creation and all its flora and fauna.

What we know about prehistoric goddess traditions comes to us from archaeological records and remnants of oral traditions, such as the 'Old Woman' in the narratives of Australia's First Peoples.

The goddess, as the divine creator, is mirrored in each woman's body; she is linked to the changing seasons, cyles of the moon, the behaviours of the animals that early people honoured, and the various observable cosmos patterns. The cycles of nature are reflected in the cycles of the female body, such as menstruation, pregnancy, birth and lactation, and menopause.

Fertile goddess, 5000 BCE
Early societies have worshipped the Fertile Goddess as the supreme repository of fertility and motherhood. The earliest proof comes from archaeological finds – paintings and figurines of women with exaggerated secondary sexual characteristics, which emphasised fertility.

Famous pieces, such as the *Venus of Lespugue* and the *Venus of Willendorf* are Upper Paleolithic (30,000–10,000 BCE) examples that may have been worshipped as goddesses. Scholars have suggested that they may have been sculpted by women looking down at their own bodies.

Ishtar, 3000 BCE
Ishtar, called the Queen of Heaven by the people of ancient Mesopotamia (modern Iraq), is the earliest historically confirmed female deity. She shared many aspects with an earlier Sumerian goddess, Inanna; the name Ishtar comes from the Semitic language of the Akkadians and is used for the goddess from about 2300 BCE on.

A multifaceted goddess, Ishtar takes three paramount forms. She is the goddess of love and sexuality, and thus, fertility; she is responsible for all life, but she is never a Mother goddess. As the goddess of war, she is often shown winged and bearing arms. Her third aspect is celestial; she is Venus, the morning and evening star.

Kali, 2000 BCE

Kali is the Sanskrit word for 'time', signifying her presence throughout the course of human life.

She is simultaneously adored and feared as she is associated with the opposing forces of creation/salvation, as well as destruction/death.

She serves as a reminder of death's inevitability, which encourages acceptance and dispels fear. She is also a goddess of fertility and time, and is called protector. As a symbol of productivity, she represents the cycles of nature, and can also be interpreted as a constant creator, taking life to give new life. As destroyer, Kali kills that which stands in the way of purity and peace in both life and death, such as evil, ignorance and egoism.

Snake Goddess, 1700–1450 BCE

This goddess is thought to have been worshipped in Crete from circa 3000–1100 BCE. Early interpretations of her worship focused on a domestic cult practised from house to palace. Subsequent excavations have revealed shrines with goddess figures located in towns or certain areas of palaces, suggesting that the sphere of the Minoan goddess extended to the official public arena.

Sophia, Biblical

Sophia, whose name in Greek means 'wisdom', is connected to the many incarnations of sacred female knowledge.

The goddess of wisdom has appeared in nearly every society

in a variety of different manifestations including Athena, Greek goddess of wisdom and military victory; Minerva, the Roman goddess of wisdom and war; Tara, the Buddhist goddess of compassion who teaches the wisdom of non-attachment; and Inanna, an early Sumerian goddess.

Sophia appears in many passages of the Bible as the female personification of wisdom, though her roles and popularity in Judaeo-Christian traditions have changed through time. She is also celebrated in Kabbalah, a form of Jewish mysticism, as the female expression of God.

In the Sistine Chapel, the female figure cradled under God's left arm in the *Creation of Adam* by Michelangelo is, in fact, Sophia, acting out her role as the female being in the creation of life and man.

Amazon, 1500–1200 BCE

According to Greek mythology, the Amazons were warrior women living north-east of Ancient Greece during the later Bronze Age, between approximately 1900 and 1200 BCE. The source of the Amazonian myths is in classical Greek literature, where they were first mentioned by Homer.

The Amazon warrior holds an important place at the dinner party, representing a tradition of powerful female warriors and the value of unified communities of women.

Hatshepsut, 1500–1458 BCE

Hatshepsut reigned over Ancient Egypt as its regent pharaoh while the official king was still too young to rule. During her reign, she adopted a role and title typically reserved for male rulers.

She was to be immensely powerful and successful as a ruler.

A series of reliefs at Deir el-Bahari recount the extraordinary commercial expeditions she undertook during her reign. Deir el-Bahari is one of the most exquisite and artistically sophisticated temples of Ancient Egypt. It stands as testament to the great construction projects developed under Hatshepsut's rule.

Despite Thutmose III's efforts to downplay her role, Hatshepsut is still widely considered to have been the legitimate fifth king of the Eighteenth Dynasty and her life as a powerful ancient female authority continues to fascinate thousands of years later. She was revitalised in Western thinking in 1882.

Judith, Biblical

It is generally accepted that the Book of Judith is ahistorical, evident from its blending of history and fiction. which is why some scholars now consider the book non-historical: a parable, a theological novel, or perhaps the first historical novel. Her quote used is from chapter 8 verse 23.

The story revolves around Judith, a daring and beautiful Jewish widow, who lived in the town of Bethulia in Israel during the sixth century BCE. When an army set siege on her town, the villain is Holofernes, a devout soldier who plans to destroy every town that does not support his king, Nebuchadnezzar. Judith uses her beauty and charm to destroy the Assyrian general and save Israel from oppression.

Judith is larger than life and she has won a place in Jewish and Christian lore, art, poetry and drama. Her name, which means 'she will be praised' or 'woman of Judaea', suggests that she represents the heroic spirit of the Jewish people, and that same spirit, as well as her chastity, have endeared her to Christianity

Owing to her unwavering religious devotion, she is able to step outside from her widow's role and dress and act in a sexually provocative manner while clearly remaining true to her ideals in the reader's mind. Her seduction and beheading of the wicked Holofernes while playing this role has been rich fodder for artists of various genres – for example, Artemisia Gentileschi.

Sappho, 630–57? BCE

Sappho was the quintessential lyric poet of ancient Greece. A nine-volume edition of Sappho's poetry was published in the third century BCE. Although the bulk of her poetry has been lost, she was well-known and greatly admired throughout antiquity as one of the greatest of lyric poets, and her immense reputation has endured through surviving fragments. While acclaimed during her lifetime, Sappho's writings were criticised and ultimately destroyed by the Church after the fourth century CE because of their erotic and lesbian imagery. The quotes used in these poems are from fragments 147 and 31, and later fragment 156.

Sappho has strengthened and changed the views of many twentieth-century women. Since her works were translated, women have used her expressions of love to enhance their own lives and others as well. Sappho remains a mysterious figure perhaps better known for introducing the terms 'lesbian' and 'sapphic' into modern vocabulary.

Aspasia of Miletus, 470–410 BCE

Aspasia was a famous woman of the ancient Greek world, known for her philosophical and rhetorical education, political influence and charm.

She arrived in Athens in the mid-440s BCE as an educated

woman, schooled by her father, Axiochus in Miletus in modern Turkey. She established an academic centre for the exchange of ideas, which served as a school for elite young women in Athens. She attracted the most prominent writers and thinkers of the time as is noted in Plutarch writings. Socrates sent his wife, to read at her salon as it rose to be one of the intellectual centres in Athens.

Aspasia became the consort of the great Classical-era Athenian statesman Pericles and bore his child. Pericles was a great orator of his time, famous for the 'Funeral Oration' recorded in Thucydides' *History of the Peloponnesian War*, which has influenced Western thought including Abraham Lincoln's *Gettysburg Address* and President Kennedy's inaugural speech.

Aspasia's life story has always been told in the shadow of Pericles' fame, but she was a woman of great eloquence and intelligence in her own right who influenced many of the writers, thinkers, and statesmen of her time and hence into the future of Western thought.

Boadaceia, 30–61 CE

Boadaceia (spelling as used by Judy Chicago) was a queen of the British Iceni tribe who led an uprising against the conquering forces of the Roman Empire in 60 or 61 CE.

It is claimed that when her husband, the peaceful king of the Iceni tribe, died, the Romans flogged her and raped her daughters. This made her rise up in rebellion.

After a series of smaller battles in which Boadaceia's troops were victorious, they met the full force of the Roman army. The Roman soldiers were far outnumbered by the rebel Celtic forces, but they were better equipped and defeated Boadaceia and her army after a long battle which Boadaceia commandeered from a chariot with her daughters. She was nearly erased from British history until Queen Victoria brought her back.

Early in the twentieth century, a bronze statue of Boadaceia and her daughters in their chariot was created in her honour and stands on the Westminster Pier in London.

Today she is a cultural symbol in Great Britain, as she stands for leadership, strength and courage against an occupying power.

Hypatia, 370–415 CE

Hypatia was a Greek Neoplatonist philosopher, astronomer and mathematician who lived in Alexandria, Egypt, then part of the Eastern Roman Empire. She was a prominent thinker of the Neoplatonic school in Alexandria, where she taught philosophy and astronomy.

She was the first woman to make significant advances in the fields of mathematics and philosophy and was also a respected teacher and astronomer.

Hypatia became a brilliant public speaker and scholar and followed her father on the library's faculty. There she wrote and lectured on mathematics and astronomy. She specialised in algebraic equations and conic sections. She invented the astrolabe used later in ship navigation and devices for measuring the density of fluids.

Her philosophy, being Neoplatonist, was seen as 'pagan' at a time of bitter religious conflict between Christians (both orthodox and 'heretical'), Jews and pagans. And the fledgling Church felt threatened not only by her as a woman speaking of this new knowledge but of the expansion of thinking. Hence she was brutally murdered and is honoured as a martyr to philosophy.

Wing Two

From now through Western history, we see the rise of patriarchy, also now designated the patricentric period, which borders with the Western civilisation process for the next five thousand years.

We are confronted with a profound reversal of values. the entire course of civilisation is seen as vitiated by patriarchy, the aggressive, plundering, male dominion of our society.

Marcella of Rome, 325–410 CE

Marcella was a saint and scholar and Christian ascetic of the Byzantine Era. She has been called the founder of monasticism. After her husband's early death, rather than remarry, as was the custom in Roman society, she espoused celibacy, devoting her life to God and the study of the Bible.

She came from a noble family and her Aventine Hill palace became a centre of Christian activity. Marcella had a strong influence on Saint Jerome, the genius who made the first translation of the Bible from Greek and Hebrew into Latin. When the Goths invaded in 410, she was brutalised, and she died of her injuries.

Most of what we know about Marcella is from a letter of Saint Jerome, written on the occasion of Marcella's death, paying tribute to her life and consoling her beloved students. In it, he says the following about his relationship with Marcella:

> How much virtue and intellect, how much holiness and purity I found in her I am afraid to say, lest I may exceed

the bounds of men's belief… This only will I say, that whatever I had gathered together by long study and by constant meditation made part of my nature, she tasted, she learned and made her own.

Note: Marcella with St Jerome (translator of the Bible from Greek and Hebrew into Latin) is often inaccurately named as his pupil rather than his colleague. We know from the letters between them that she often engaged in scholarship with him, questioned his arguments and was never afraid to criticise him, treating him as her equal.

Saint Bridget of Ireland, 450–525 CE

Bridget (Brigid), a modern Irish saint, was a determined, faithful Catholic who was responsible for founding convents and monasteries throughout Ireland. Bridget's Celtic name, Brigid, which means 'fiery arrow', can be traced back to the goddess of the same name with whom Bridget is often conflated. Before the appropriation of the early Catholic Church, she was Cailleach, a feminine creator deity, also known as Queen of Winter in Gaelic mythology.

The most recognised saints in Ireland, Bridget and Saint Patrick, are the main Irish saints to hold a place on the celebrated Catholic Calendar of Saints.

The lore of Brigid is particularly interesting because it demonstrates the adaptation of Celtic and pagan beliefs, using ancient Celtic festivals like Imbolc, to Christianity. Bridget is equated with her pagan counterpart, Brigid, who was the Celtic goddess of poetry, healing and metal arts.

Today she is remembered all over Ireland with the famous *muiredach* cross, the Celtic cross of the tenth century.

Theodora, 500–545 CE

Before rising to the throne as empress of the Byzantine Empire, Theodora's life had been exceedingly humble. Her father's early death led her to become an 'actress', a term synonymous with a prostitute in modern day.

The events that mark this period of her life were first described by Procopius of Caesarea, the most eminent historian of the age who was a misogynist so it is a biased history.

When Theodora married Justin in 527, it was called the love story of the ages. A few years later, they were made the emperor (Augustus) and empress of the eastern Roman world. However, Empress Theodora never forgot from where she came. She gives us a 'rags to riches' story.

Empress Theodora made her mark in three different areas: the strengthening of the institution of marriage, the banishment of prostitution and the provision of welfare for those who were traumatised.

She was always an advocate for women. Lynda Garland (1999) states, 'much of Emperor Justin's legislation was concerned with protecting women and their rights'.

Theodora was aware that violence against women and girls was hidden, ignored and accepted. She reformed legislations concerning the status and the protection of women.

She is remembered in many outstanding mosaics sitting with Justin with her maids in waiting. In Ravenna on the north-east coast of Italy, the mosaics are still enjoyed for their sheer beauty.

It has been argued that her feminist spirit was based on the following phrase from Virgil's *Aeneid*: 'No stranger to misfortune myself, I have learned to receive the sufferings of others.'

Hrosvitha, 935–1002 CE

Hrosvitha was the earliest known woman poet in Germany, and some scholars even consider her the first female dramatist, or playwright, since ancient times.

Of noble Saxon birth, she entered a Benedictine monastery in Gandersheim in Saxony (modern-day Germany) as a canoness. Some of her early years may have been spent in King Otto's court.

She found inspiration in Terence the Roman playwright, who wrote of sex but whose work trumpeted the fragility of the female sex, writing of debauchery and lust in sexual encounters.

Hrosvitha wrote from a woman's point of view and challenged Terence's misogyny. Her lost *Epics* comprised a history on the life of Otto I, the King of the Germans and Holy Roman Emperor who lived from 912 to 973, and a history of Gandersheim Abbey. Hrosvitha's works are impressive in their expository scope, referencing the works of Virgil, Ovid and other ancient poets.

Trota of Salerno, circa 1097

Trota (Trotula) was an eleventh-century Italian doctor regarded as world's first gynaecologist. Her many achievements in the male-dominant area of gynaecology both educated her contemporaries and advanced progressive ideas about women's health care.

She served as a physician and professor at the medical school in Salerno, Italy, the first medical school in the world, where knowledge was garnered from the Islamic world and not impeded by the imposed dark ages of the west. Her husband and sons were also doctors at the school.

She advocated for the use of opiates during labour, opposing the Christian belief of the time that women should experience a maximum of suffering during childbirth as punishment for Eve's sin.

Trota revolutionised the medical field by suggesting men could also be infertile.

Her manuscripts first published in Latin in the twelfth century circulated the pre-modern world. From my research, I have reason to believe Hildegard of Bingen was influenced by her writings. These women born into the renaissance of the eleventh century, had more opportunities living before the time of the age of witch trials, which ran between 1550 and 1700, in the Reformation and Counter Reformation.

Modern research is unravelling her original writings from the composite Trotula texts rediscovered in 1985. (Trotula has referred to a group of texts on women's medicine dating from the twelfth century.)

Eleanor of Aquitaine, 1122–1204

Eleanor, Queen of France was the wife of King Louis VII and later Queen of England as the wife of King Henry II and mother of two future kings. She lived a long life of many contrasts of splendour and desolation, power and peril.

Estranged from King Henry, she was imprisoned by him for supporting the revolt of her son against him. A tireless political fighter and a born survivor, the humbled queen emerged from sixteen years of imprisonment, age sixty-seven, to rule England with wisdom and panache during the absence of her son King Richard the Lionheart, while he fought in the ruinous Third Crusade. When Henry died in 1189, she was released by her son Richard I.

We know from correspondence with Hildegard of Bingen that Eleanor had times of despondency and was encouraged by Hildegard.

The most forward-thinking academics write that Eleanor was a woman firmly grounded in the culture of her time, and while formidable and intelligent, she wasn't exceptional when set against other high-ranking ruling women of her period. The twelfth century in general is readily accessible today because it was a time of burgeoning scholarship that is now regarded the first renaissance. However, most writings in this Medieval time were not written as historical narratives or analyses but as moral tales to illustrate the workings of God in their time.

One of the things that fascinates historians about Eleanor was the amount of energy she had and how indefatigable she was right up until her last days. Chadwick says, 'she died at the age of 82, which was a marvellous span in a period without life-saving operations and medication. Most octogenarians, even the robust ones, these days are swallowing many tablets to keep them up to scratch.'

Finally, the signing of the Magna Carta by her son King John in 1215 was a turning point and influence for the betterment of the Western world.

Hildegard of Bingen, 1098–1179

Hildegard of Bingen was a German Benedictine abbess, writer, composer, philosopher, mystic, visionary and polymath of the High Middle Ages, a time of renaissance.

Hildegard is one of the best-known composers of sacred music as well as being, now the most recorded in modern history.

She wrote theology treatises, two science and health books,

many biographies and thousands of letters to kings, bishops, popes, and emperors of her day. She built an abbey in the Rhine Valley, which became a hub of learning, healing and exchange of ideas with an infirmary for the sick and dying, apothecary for herbs and healing and scriptorium for writing and copying books and music.

All her life she faced the power of patriarchy, misogyny and sexism from the hierarchy of the male-controlled church that worked to silence her and hold her back at every forward step she took.

Petronilla de Meath, 1300–1324

Petronilla de Meath was the first Irish woman to be burned at the stake for the crime of heresy.

She served as a maid to Lady Alice Kyteler, one of the earliest women to be accused of witchcraft who because of her money and position was able to flee Ireland. Unfortunately, this left her workers and servants, including Petronilla de Meath, to face the fury and wrath of the accusers and the Bishop of Ossory, Richard de Ledrede. Petronilla was the first woman burnt at the stake for heresy, and it was the first known trial to treat women practising witchcraft as an organised group.

Petronilla serves as a first of the many women tried and convicted of witchcraft during the Middle Ages.

Christine de Pizan, 1365–1430

Christine de Pizan was an Italian-French late medieval author. Her works, considered to be some of the earliest feminist writings, include poetry, novels, biography and autobiography, as well as literary, political and religious commentary. She completed forty-one works during her thirty-year career from 1399 to 1429.

She became the first woman in France, and possibly Europe, to earn a living solely by writing. She had spent most of her childhood and all of her adult life in Paris and then the abbey at Poissy and wrote entirely in her adopted language, Middle French. She married in 1380 at the age of fifteen and was widowed ten years later. Some of the impetus for her writing came from her need to earn a living to support her mother, a niece and her two surviving children.

She served as a court writer for several dukes (Louis of Orleans, Philip the Bold of Burgundy and John the Fearless of Burgundy) and the French royal court during the reign of Charles VI.

In recent decades, Christine's work has been returned to prominence by the efforts of scholars such as Charity Cannon Willard, and Simone de Beauvoir. Certain scholars have argued that she should be seen as an early feminist who efficiently used language to convey that women could play an important role within society.

Her writing was instrumental in introducing the concept of equality and justice for women in medieval France.

Isabella d'Este, 1474–1539

Isabella d'Este was a powerful and well-educated political woman, humanitarian, patron of the arts and mother of seven. She was Marchioness of Mantua, a leading and most influential women of the Italian Renaissance as a major cultural and political figure. As a leader of fashion, her innovative style of dressing was copied by women throughout Italy and at the French court.

She studied ancient Greek and Roman language and history. and was well educated.

In 1509, her husband Francesco was captured by the forces of King Charles VIII of France and held in Venice as a prisoner. In his absence, Isabella served as regent, defending the city as commander of the city's forces. She negotiated a peace treaty that provided for her husband's safe return in 1512.

Wealth and education gave Isabella the opportunity to prove the ability of a woman in the middle ages of patriarch history, a time when many were being burnt at the stake for rising above the tide.

Elizabeth I, 1533–1603
Elizabeth I, Queen of England and Ireland and a member of the Tudor family, was a revered English queen. She ascended to the throne at a time when England was in religious conflict and economic hardship.

She ruled over a period of English history often referred to as 'The Golden Age'.

Sometimes called the Virgin Queen, Gloriana or Good Queen Bess, Elizabeth was the last of the five monarchs of the house of Tudor. The Elizabethan era was a time of relative religious freedom.

In 1559, Queen Elizabeth's coronation was closely followed by the Acts of Supremacy and Uniformity. The former constituted a reversal of her sister Mary Queen of Scots' attempt to restore England to the Catholic Church.

Elizabeth earned her country's respect as a bold and independently minded ruler, who successfully lifted England out of its troubled state.

Artemisia Gentileschi, 1593–1652
Artemisia Gentileschi was an Italian baroque painter, now con-

sidered one of the most accomplished seeventeenth-century artists, initially working in the style of Caravaggio.

She was producing professional work by the age of fifteen and turned the horrors of her own life – repression, injustice, rape – into brutal biblical paintings that were also a war cry for oppressed women. Her innovative compositions and focus on biblical heroines set her apart from her male contemporaries and have led to the celebration of Gentileschi as a painter with a uniquely female perspective.

She was forgotten as an artist for 450 years as the history of art was written by men. Only now is she being rediscovered and understood.

Anna Maria van Schurman, 1607–1678

Anna Maria van Schurman was a German-born Dutch scholar, philosopher and poet and artist, best known for her defence of female education.

She was the most highly educated woman of the seventeenth century. She received a strong classical education from her father. Considered a child prodigy, she could read and translate both Latin and Greek by the age of seven and had learned German, French, Hebrew, English, Spanish and Italian by age eleven. She also studied art and became a distinguished artist in the fields of drawing, painting, and etching, though few examples of her art exist today.

At the age of twenty-nine, after years of advocating for women's education, she was invited to attend the University of Utrecht as the first female student. The administration required that she sit behind a curtain in class, as they believed she would distract the male students. She graduated with a degree in law – the first female graduate.

Anna Maria participated in contemporary intellectual discourse, communicating with important cultural figures, such as the philosopher René Descartes,

She published articles detailing the ways in which women's brains functioned as effectively as a men's and the damage that occurred to women's abilities if they were only considered capable of being wives and mothers.

Wing Three

Patriarchy is a society based on the absolute of the male gender. This became entrenched in all spheres from supreme centres of prestige along with the Church and down. Any challenge to this authority was questioned, suppressed or punished.

Anne Hutchinson, 1591–1643

Anne Hutchison was an American Puritan spiritist. She travelled from England to Massachusetts Bay Colony to find freedom from religious pressure only to find more suppression. She preached to both women and men, questioned Puritan teachings on salvation, believing women also had possibility of salvation, and she challenged the domination of male authority and gender roles.

The Puritan leader John Winthrop saw her as a dangerous woman. He had her charged with dishonouring the Puritan fathers and holding Bible meetings in her home and had her sent to trial.

She debated the magistrates, all men, who accused her. Their convictions were so weak she won every debate against them in the courtroom. She was still sentenced and dismissed from her community and home.

The Salem Witch Hunts were still to begin! It is said the motivating force to establish Harvard College for men at that time was to strengthen Puritan views and men's ability to debate.

Sentenced and shunned, she walked to a new territory in an area called Rhode Island with seventy followers, making her the first woman to co-found an American colony. She was accidentally killed in a misunderstanding with the Indian tribes living in the area.

The government of Massachusetts pardoned Anne in 1986 nearly 350 years after her tragic death.

She is titled one of the early American feminists.

Sacajawea, 1788–1812?
Sacajawea was the daughter of a Shoshone chief, captured by an enemy tribe and sold to a French Canadian trapper who made her his wife at age twelve. At sixteen, she was taken as interpreter and negotiator on the Lewis and Clark Expedition (1803–1806) to discover a route through the North American west to the Pacific Ocean. She was an essential member of the expedition but not recognised until recent years. Both Native American legend and journals from the Lewis and Clark expedition reference her important contribution briefly.

As the journey began along the river, they quickly needed Sacajawea's skills and language to negotiate with inland tribes for horses needed for mountain crossings. Without her presence, they would not have achieved their chartered mission of exploring the Louisiana Territory.

Unlike the men, Sacajawea did not receive honour or payment for this successful expedition.

In an era in which women, particularly Native American women, were considered either weak and helpless or dangerous, Sacajawea proved to be an icon of bravery and adventure amongst men who were renowned for such traits.

Today she has been rediscovered as a well-known and respected Native American women. She stands not only as a symbol of the strength of Native American women, but as an emblem of the tenacity and power of all women.

Caroline Lucretia Herschel, 1750–1848

Caroline Herschel was a German astronomer whose most significant contributions to astronomy were her discoveries of eight comets, including the periodic comet 35P/Herschel-Rigollet, which bears her name. She was the younger sister of astronomer William Herschel, who worked at the court in Bath, England, and with whom she worked throughout her career.

She was the first woman to receive a salary as a scientist; the first woman in England to hold a government position; and the first woman to publish scientific findings in the Philosophical Transactions of the Royal Society, and to be named an Honorary Member of the Royal Astronomical Society. The King of Prussia presented her with a Gold Medal for Science on her ninety-sixth birthday (1846).

Her achievements enabled generations of women to develop a career in the sciences, a field that was once exclusively reserved for men.

Mary Wollstonecraft, 1759–1883

Mary Wollstonecraft was a renowned women's rights activist who authored *A Vindication of the Rights of Woman*, 1792, a classic of rationalist feminism that is considered the earliest and most important treatise advocating equality for women. This essay is often seen as the foundation of modern women's rights movements in the Western world.

She argued that women are not naturally inferior to men, but appear to be only because they lack education. She suggested that both men and women should be treated as rational beings and imagined a social order founded on reason and equality.

Until the late twentieth century, Mary's life was encompassed by several unconventional personal relationships which received more attention than her writing. Today she is regarded as one of the founding feminist philosophers. Feminists today often cite both her life and her works as important influences.

She died in 1797 during the birth of her second daughter, Mary, who in 1816, as Mary Shelley, published her own masterpiece, *Frankenstein*.

Sojourner Truth, 1797–1883
Sojourner Truth was an American abolitionist and women's rights activist. She was born into slavery in the backstreets of New York but escaped with her infant daughter to freedom in 1826. After going to court to recover her son in 1828, she became the first black woman to win such a case against a white man.

She gave herself the name Sojourner Truth in 1843 after she became convinced that God had called her to leave the city and go into the countryside 'testifying the hope that was in her'.

Her best-known speech was delivered in 1851 at the Women's Rights Convention in Ohio. The speech became widely known during the Civil War by the title 'Ain't I a Woman?', a variation of the original speech rewritten by someone else using a stereotypical Southern dialect, whereas Sojourner Truth was from New York and grew up speaking Dutch as her first language

She was one of the first to articulate the similarities between the struggles of black slaves and the struggles of women and was a powerful force in their fight for justice and equality. She met Abraham Lincoln and helped freed slaves find jobs and build new lives – the beginning of the challenge to segregation.

Her last words were 'Lord, I have done my duty, and I have told the whole truth and kept nothing back.'

Susan B. Anthony, 1820–1906
Susan B. Anthony was an American social reformer and women's rights activist. She became the face of the American suffrage movement and one of its primary organisers. Her actions contributed to significant progress in the inclusion of women in the United States political process.

Born into a Quaker family, she collected anti-slavery petitions at the age of seventeen. In 1856, she became the New York state agent for the American Anti-Slavery Society.

In 1850, women were not included in educational options, could not own property, had no legal rights and were subservient to men.

Some of Susan's inspiration came from meeting kindred spirits – women like Elizabeth Cady Stanton. Elizabeth was the writer of many speeches but tied down with seven children. It was Susan B. Anthony who became the face and voice of the suffragists and also the martyr of suffrage.

Together they prepared 'The Declaration of Women's Rights' to be read at the centenary celebration of 1876. When refused, they stood at the entrance and handed out printed copies as the delegates were leaving. In her best gown, Susan stood up in the bandstand and megaphoned to the crowds swarming out.

In 1872, Susan voted illegally and was charged and found guilty, the judge writing up the verdict before the trial! She was fined $100, which she refused to pay: 'I will never pay a penny of this unjust penalty.' The judge waived it, preventing it from going to the High Court.

Susan died fourteen years before the vote for women was won. In August 2020, the centenary of women getting the vote, Susan B. Anthony was acknowledged and pardoned from the charge of 1872.

Elizabeth Blackwell, 1821–1910

Elizabeth Blackwell was a British physician, notable as the first woman to receive a medical degree in the United States and the first woman on the Medical Register of the General Medical Council.

She played an important role in both the United States and the United Kingdom as she championed the participation of women in the medical profession and ultimately opened her own medical college for women in London. She pioneered and promoted education for women in medicine, and was a social awareness and moral reformer.

She faced the difficulties of blocks. The only way she got a foot in a medical school door was because it did not designate 'men' – it took it for granted and she challenged them. It needed a vote of the 120 men to say 'yes' for her to enter. After she graduated, hospitals would not accept her as an intern and she only graduated by 'knowing' someone. She faced much humiliation and set up ways to make it easier for future women.

Her contributions remain celebrated with the Elizabeth Blackwell Medal, awarded annually to a woman who has made significant contribution to the promotion of women in medicine.

Emily Dickinson, 1830–1886

Emily Dickinson is one of America's greatest and most original poets. She challenged the existing definitions of poetry and the poet's work. She experimented with expression in order to free it from conventional restraints and crafted a new type of persona for the first person. The speakers in Dickinson's poetry are sharp-sighted observers who see the inescapable limitations of their societies as well as their imagined and imaginable escapes.

Emily defied the nineteenth-century expectation that women were to be demure and obedient to men. Her honest and uninhibited writing made her an early feminist voice, even as she maintained an outward appearance of submissiveness.

Her poems normally do not have titles but go by numbers and in this poem I have used No. 258, 509 from *The Complete Poems* edited by Thomas H Johnson. Of the other quotes, the first is from the minister at her girls' seminary and the second from the editor of the day at the *Springfield Republican* local paper.

> This is my letter to the World
> That never wrote to Me –
> The simple News that Nature told –
> With tender Majesty   No. 441

Dame Ethel Mary Smyth, 1858–1944

Ethel Smyth was a twentieth-century English composer, champion of women's rights and female musicians and a member of the women's suffrage movement. During her lifetime, she composed symphonies, choral works and operas including *The Wreckers*, 1906. She is noted for 'The March of Women', a battle cry for the women's suffrage movement.

Smyth and her ardent feminist friend Emmeline Pankhurst were arrested in London along with a hundred other suffragettes for throwing stones at the houses of suffrage opponents; she was imprisoned for two months in Holloway prison.

Smyth tended to be marginalised as a 'woman composer', as though her work could not be accepted as mainstream. Yet when she produced more delicate compositions, they were criticised for not measuring up to the standard of her male competitors. George Bernard Shaw wrote to her after her Mass in D was performed at the Royal Albert Hall, 'It was your music that cured me for ever of the old delusion that women could not do man's work in art and in all other things…your Mass will stand up in the biggest company! Magnificent!'

In 1922, she was named a Dame of the British Empire, the first female composer to be so honoured.

Margaret Sanger, 1879–1966

Margaret Sanger is known as an American birth control activist, sex educator, writer and nurse. Margaret Sanger saw reproductive freedom as a class issue and sought to educate working-class women about these topics.

She popularised the term 'birth control', opened the first birth control clinic in the United States, and established organisations that evolved into the Planned Parenthood Federation of America.

The first quote is from *Time* magazine, 1932.

She challenged New York's Comstock laws, which banned the dissemination of information about contraception to women. She created her own newspaper, *The Woman Rebel*, to inform the public and distributed it and other pamphlets on sex and birth control. The paper was banned.

She was charged with inciting murder by circulating literature to advocate birth control. She asserted the pamphlets were informative 'to cure and prevent disease'. In February 1915, she fled to England to avoid going to gaol.

Today Margaret's reputation faces the challenges of navigating the tricky terrain of the interface between social reform and political power. Her work has been falsely described as a type of racism and her name and reputation have been caught up in the movement to dishonour names and take down statues, as well as a move to override Roe versus Wade by a very conservative Supreme Court.

Natalie Clifford Barney, 1876–1972

Natalie Barney was both a poet and a prose writer, famous for her weekly salons. Her Friday Salon, held in 20 rue Jacob on the Paris left bank for more than sixty years, gathered together many of the twentieth century's greatest artists and writers from the Western world, including many leading figures in French literature along with American and British modernists of the Lost Generation.

She is celebrated for openly living and writing as a lesbian during a time when women's behaviour was closely circumscribed.

She worked to promote women writing and formed L'Académie des Femmes in response to the all-male French Academy. She began publishing love poems under her own name as early as 1900. She wrote in both French and English. In her writings, she supported feminism and pacifism and opposed monogamy.

Virginia Woolf, 1882–1941

Virginia Woolf was a renowned British novelist associated with the modernist movement in literature; her writing characterised by experiments in language, narrative and the treatment of time. Woolf is often considered one of the most innovative writers of the twentieth century. In her work, she discusses the issues and prejudices surrounding women's writing in the Western world.

During the interwar period, Woolf was a significant figure in London literary society and a member of the Bloomsbury Group. Her most famous works include the novels *Mrs Dalloway*, *The Waves*, *To the Lighthouse*, *Orlando* and the book-length essay, 'A Room of One's Own' (1929), with its famous dictum, 'A woman must have money and a room of her own if she is to write fiction.'

Now one of the most revered icons of twentieth-century feminism, Woolf has been celebrated not only for her fiction and non-fiction works but also in popular culture. Her introduction of new narrative methods and her encouragement of women's writing have resulted in a wealth of still-treasured literature that continues to inspire generations of readers, writers and scholars.

Georgia O'Keeffe, 1887–1986

Georgie O'Keeffe was a well known American painter and considered by some to be the mother of the feminist art movement.

She worked in a discipline dominated by male artists, critics, gallery owners and curators who were critical of women artists. Despite these obstacles, Georgia O'Keeffe launched a successful career, developing a distinctive painting style that employed organic vulvar forms and floral imagery.

Her life experiences influenced her art; imagery from her time in New York and New Mexico reappears in her painting.

Since the 1920s, her work has become popular with the feminist movement and its reclamation and rediscovery of women's history.

The Georgia O'Keeffe Museum, the first museum in the United States dedicated to a single female artist, opened in 1997 in Santa Fe, New Mexico. It houses 1,149 of her works.

In talking about her work, O'Keeffe said, 'The men liked to put me down as the best woman painter. I think I'm one of the best painters' (Chadwick, *Women, Art, and Society*, 303).

Today the new mode of ecological consciousness now emerging sees this period of the earth community as having a basic nurturing aspect that tends more towards traditional feminine than masculine qualities.

The challenge is ongoing. There are still many injustices enacted against women. Domestic violence is at an all-time high. Movements like #metoo# timesup encourage women to use their voices and hold patriarchal systems and individuals accountable.

Judy Chicago

Judy Chicago is an artist, author, feminist, educator, and intellectual whose career now spans five decades. Her influence both within and beyond the art community is attested to by her inclusion in hundreds of publications and exhibitions throughout the world.

In addition to a life of prodigious art making, Chicago is the author of numerous books: *Through the Flower: My Struggle as a Woman Artist,* 1975; *The Dinner Party: A Symbol of Our Heritage,* 1979; *Embroidering Our Heritage: The Dinner Party Needlework,* 1985 (Anchor/Doubleday); *Holocaust Project: From Darkness into Light,* 1993.

Chicago remains steadfast in her commitment to the power of art as a vehicle for intellectual transformation and social change and to women's right to engage in the highest level of art production. As a result, she has become a symbol for people everywhere, known and respected as an artist, writer, teacher, feminist and humanist whose work and life are models for an enlarged definition of art, an expanded role for the artist, and women's right to freedom of expression.

Bibliography

Primary Sources

Bancroft, Anne, *Weavers of Wisdom: Women Mystics of the Twentieth Century.* Penguin Books, London, 1989

Barnstone, Willis, *Sweetbitter Love: Poems of Sappho.* (Trans.) Shambhala, Boston & London, 2006

Berry, Thomas, *The Dream of the Earth.* Sierra Club, San Fransisco CA, 1988 (helped me with the invention of the eye with which to see our evolving world and its large celebration of existence)

Berresford Ellis, Peter, *Celtic Women, Women in Celtic Society and Literature.* Constable& Co, London, 1995

Butcher, Carmen Acevedo, Letter to Eleanor Queen of England, cited in Butcher, Carmen Acevedo, *St. Hildegard of Bingen: Doctor of the Church.* Paraclete Press, 2013

Caprio, Betsy, *Woman Sealed in the Tower.* Paulist Press, NJ, 1982

Chadwick, Elizabeth, *Eleanor of Aquitaine: Going the Distance*

Chicago, Judy, *The Dinner Party, Restoring Women to History.* The Monacelli Press, 2014

Collins, Billy, *Taking off Emily Dickinson's Clothes.* from Selected Poems of the same title, Picador, London, 1988

Cosman, Carol, Keefe, Joan, Weaver, Kathleen, *The Penguin Book of Women Poems.* Allen Lane, 1978

DeSalvo, Louise and Leaska, M. *The Letters of Vita Sackville-West and Virginia Woolf.* Cleis Press, San Francisco, 1984

Dickinson, Emily, *My Life had stood a loaded gun.* (Ed. Martin Secker, 1933) Penguin Random House UK, 2016

—, *The Complete poems.* (Ed. Thomas H. Johnson) Faber & Faber, 1970

Freeman, Phillip, *Searching for Sappho: The Lost Songs and World of the First Woman Poet.* W.W. Norton, London, 2016

Gerhard, Jane F., 'From Controversy to Canonization: The Dinner Party's Journey to Brooklyn', from *The Dinner Party*. The Monacello Press, 2014

Harding, Lesley and Mimmocchi, Denise, *O'Keeffe, Preston, Cossington Smith: Making Modernism*. Heide Museum of Modern Art for Art Gallery of NSW, 2017

Hart, Ellen Louise and Smith, Martha Nell, *Open Me Carefully: Emily Dickinson's Intimate letters to Susan Dickinson*. Paris Press, 1998

Healey, Judith Koll, *The Lost Letters Aquitaine*. Harper Collins USA, 2004

Heer, Friedrich, *Medieval World Europe 1100–1350*. Weidenfeld, London, 1993.

Hildegard of Bingen, *Book of Divine Works with Letters and Songs*. (Ed. Matthew Fox) Bear & Co., 1987

Hoskin, Michael, 'Caroline Herschel: "the unquiet heart"', *Endeavour*, Vol. 29, No. 1, March 2005

Kenyon, Olga, *800 Years of Women's Letters*. Alan Sutton, UK, 1992

Keating, Colleen, *Hildegard of Bingen: A poetic journey*. Ginninderra Press, Port Adelaide, 2019

Pinkola, Clarissa Estés, *Women who run with the Wolves*. Random House, London, 1992

Saxby, Maurice & Ingpen, Robert, *The Great Deeds of Heroic Women*. Millennium Books, NSW, 1990

Sjöö, Monica & Mor, Barbara, *The Great Cosmic Mother: Rediscovering the Religion of the Earth*. Harper, San Francisco, 1991 (a story about humanity's heritage)

Weir, Alison, *Eleanor of Aquitaine*. Ballantine, 1999

Woolf, Virginia, *A Room of One's Own*. Grafton Books, Collins Publishing, London, 1977 (First published by the Hogarth Press Ltd, 1929)

Online

ABC Classic – *Composers* – Ethel Smyth, February 2020

ABC Classic – Hildegard of Bingen: life and music of the great female composer and top 100 composers of the Western World

Brown, Mark, 'Mary Wollstonecraft's statue becomes one of 2020's most polarising artworks', *The Guardian*, 25 December 2020

Brooklyn Museum, Elizabeth A. Sackler Centre for Feminist Art: Place Settings

Caroline Herschel – StarChild www.starchily.gsfc.nasa.gov/docs

Michals, Debra, 'Anne Hutchinson', National Women's History Museum, 2015.

Rizzo, Johanna, Sacajawea from Women Heroes, National Geographic.com

www.womenshistory.org/education-resources/biographies/anne-hutchinson

The following, and Wikipedia, were used as a way of becoming familiar with many of the women

www.biography.com

www.britannica.com

www.the-history-girls-blogspot.com

www.poetryfoundation.org

Discography

A Feather on the Breath of God: Sequences and Hymns by Abbess Hildegard of Bingen, Hyperion, 1981

'March of the Women', by Ethyl Smyth, YouTube from The Lost Women of Music, 2019

Illustrations

Page 11: Judy Chicago, *The Dinner Party* 1974–1979; photo Donald Woodman

Page 13: from a fresco of Sappho holding writing implements from Pompeii Naples, Archaeological Museum, Wikimedia Commons

Page 43: 11th–12th century Latin codex: (self-portrait) Visions of Hildegard von Bingen

Page 77: young Elizabeth Blackwell, archives: University of Bristol (bristol.ac.uk)

www.ingramcontent.com/pod-product-compliance
Lightning Source LLC
Chambersburg PA
CBHW071503080526
44587CB00014B/2194